NoSlang.com

Internet Slang Dictionary

By Ryan Jones

www.noslang.com

Internet Slang Dictionary

Dedicated to all the parents who sometimes feel like their kids are speaking a foreign language online.

First Edition
ISBN: 978-1-84728-752-6
Printed in the USA
Cover design by Jon Eddy

Disclaimer

About the Author

Ryan Jones is a software engineer from the Detroit, Michigan area. He graduated from the University of Michigan with a bachelors in computer science and enjoys hockey, poker, philosophy, and internet culture. Ryan runs several websites and has written articles for several websites, books, and magazines.

Please send any errata, suggestions, feedback, compliments, donations, hate mail, or praise to ryan@noslang.com

Introduction

"Many kids, when online, seem to forget all the rules they were ever taught. They feel somewhat invincible and free to say what they want to whom they want. The more they talk online the more at ease they feel and the more comfortable they get in their new online world. In this world they are in control, not their parents. Unfortunately, most parents are not in control when it comes to internet usage in their home. Our kids generally have more experience with computers and are very comfortable with them, while most parents are still trying to figure out how to program the VCR our kids are creating their own web sites."

Richard French *TheParentsEdge.com*

As a concerned parent you try to stay on top of what your kids are doing on the internet, but sometimes the technological gap can be hard to overcome. The online lingo is evolving everyday and unless you're itk (in the know) you can easily get confused.

The first step in protecting your children is to take an active role in what they're doing online. This can be a difficult task if you don't understand what they're saying. This book will be your most valuable tool in breaking that code.

My goal is to teach you the internet language. After reading this book you'll know that when somebody says NIFOC to your daughter and she franticly types p911, you can tell the person to GTHA and LOL because you know she's safe with MOS.

3

Table of Contents

Common techniques used in creating slang
Is internet slang helping or hurting our youth?
Other useful internet slang resources.
Some tips for keeping your kids safe on the net.
Common sense rules for kids on the net.

What is Internet Slang?

As the internet became embedded in pagers, cell phones, and other smaller devices, people found it increasingly difficult to type on smaller keyboards. They soon realized that the less they had to type the more they could say, and the quicker they could say it. There was a definite need for a shortcut.

Internet slang is the broad definition given to almost any acronym or abbreviation created to eliminate keystrokes online (whether it's IM, email, chat, or text message). Unlike spoken slang, internet slang is much harder to learn. That's why I created NoSlang.com (and later this book); to help people understand the internet's ever evolving language.

Some internet slang dates all the way back to World War II, but most of it is made up "on the fly" by removing vowels from words or taking the first letter of multiple words. There's no set rule for how to create internet slang, and many teens tend to use whatever is most convenient.

Where is Slang Used?

Originally, internet slang was reserved for chat rooms like IRC (internet relay chat), AOL (America Online), or Yahoo. Lately however, slang has spread to instant messaging programs and cell phone text messages. In fact, more and more teachers are reporting seeing words like "lol" in homework assignments, and some circles of friends have even starting saying things like "lol", "wtf" and "brb" out loud.

Acronyms Vs. Abbreviations

If you're like me, the slight difference in meaning between an acronym and an abbreviation carries little to no significance. Many of my readers however, have emailed me to discuss my use of the HTML <acronym> tag. If you're a true NoSlang.com diehard you'll remember that my blog discussed changing from using the <acronym> tag to using the <abbr> tag instead. As my readers correctly pointed out, slang only qualifies as an acronym if it uses the first letter of multiple words to make another pronounceable word (like NASA, or SCUBA). Anything else only qualifies as an abbreviation, or the shortening of a word.

An argument can be made that some tough to pronounce (but theoretically possible) internet slang like "lol" can be an acronym, however slang like "brb" or "idk" wouldn't qualify as acronyms because even though they use the first letter of words they stand for, they aren't new words in themselves (and good luck pronouncing them).

How to Speak L33t

L33t speak (often called Leet, 1337, or l337) is the practice of replacing letters in words with numbers or symbols that look like that letter. For example, an 'a' might be replaced with @, 'b' might be replaced with the two characters '|3', or a 'T' might be replaced with a '7'. The word l33t comes from the word 'elite', and is mostly an internet "I'm cooler than you" type concept. There are no real rules for l33t, so technically it could be considered more of a code than a language.

L33t started out in chat rooms and bulletin board systems like IRC and Usenet, but lately is more likely to be found in multiplayer online games like Counter Strike or World of Warcraft. Leet's original purpose was to hide content from bulletin board moderators. Moderators would search for terms like "porn", "wares" (short for software), or "exploits" so they could remove them from their networks. To combat this, early "hackers" would change the spelling so their posts wouldn't be easily found. To better hide content, porn became pr0n, wares (also called warez) became w4r3z, and exploits became spl01tz. Those who knew what to look for could still find it easily while the site administrators struggled.

To this day computers (and parents) still have a hard time understanding l33t. In fact, may network administrators urge their users to use l33t for their passwords. Simply changing "diet soda" to "d13t s0d4" can create a very memorable, but extremely hard to crack password.

To help the reader better understand l33t, we've included the common l33t letters next to each letter in it's dictionary section.

Single Letter Words

Single letter word replacements are used so frequently online that I felt they should have their own section in the book. You should probably memorize this list, as often times these letters are added to other slang to form new words. By learning these you'll not only be able to understand current slang, but create your own as well.

B	be
C	see
K	ok
O	oh
M	am
R	are
U	you
2	two, too, or to
4	for

A Note On Swearing…

As you browse through this book you may have noticed some offensive words. I struggled for a long time with whether or not to *** them out, and after a long and lengthy discussion I decided to replace some of the bad words with ***s.

It was a tough decision, and it's not one I'd normally make. It's always been my belief that in some cases swear words are necessary to convey the true meaning of the writing regardless of how offensive they may be. After all, when teens use sayings like WTF they aren't actually saying "What the freak?"

Top 25 Slang Terms For Parents

In an effort to help you get up to speed on internet slang, I've included my list of the top 25 slang terms that all parents should know. How many of these words can you identify? Chances are your kids have actually used many of them in their daily online conversations.

ASL(R P)	Age Sex Location (Race / Picture)
BF / GF	Boyfriend / Girlfriend
BRB	Be Right Back
CD9	Code 9 - means parents are around
GNOC	Get Naked on Cam (webcam)
GTG	Got to Go
IDK	I don't know
(L)MIRL	(Lets) meet in real life
LOL	Laugh Out Loud
MorF	Male or Female
MOS	Mom Over Shoulder
NIFOC	Naked in Front of Computer
Noob	Newbie – (insult) new person / player
NMU	Not much, you?
P911	Parent Emergency
PAW	Parents are Watching
PIR	Parent In Room
POS	Parent Over Shoulder
PRON	Porn
PRW	Parents Are Watching
S2R	Send To Receive (pictures)
TDTM	Talk Dirty To Me
Warez	Pirated Software
W/E	Whatever
WTF	What the f**k?

Numbers & Symbols

^	up
*4u	kiss for you
*67	unknown
0day	software obtained before release
10q	thank you
10x	thanks
12b	wannabe
1337	elite
13itch	bit*h
143	I love you
1ab	wannabe
2b	to be
2day	today

2gether	together
2h4u	too hot for you
2m	tomorrow
2moro	tomorrow
2morrow	tomorrow
2moz	tomorrow
2mz	tomorrow
2nite	tonight
2sday	Tuesday
2tali	totally
2tm	to the max
31337	elite
313373	elite
31EE7	elite
3q	thank you

3u	thank you
4col	for crying out loud
4eva	forever
4ever	forever
4get	forget
4gv	forgive
4ker	f**ker
4king	f**king
4lyf3	for life
4lyfe	for life
4q	f**k you
4tw	for the win
4u	for you
5-oh	cop
53x	sex

5n	fine
6flx	sex flick
6up	cops in area
6y	sexy
8008135	boobies
<3	love
?u@	where are you?
?up	what's up?
?^	what's up?
@	at
@$$	a**
^5	high five

A a @ /-\ 4

a/s/l	age sex location
a/s/l/r	age sex location race
aaf	as a friend
aamof	as a matter of fact
acc	account
ack	acknowledged
addy	address
adn	any day now
afaic	as far as I'm concerned
afaics	as far as I can see
afaict	as far as I can tell
afaik	as far as I know
afair	as far as I recall

afc	away from computer
afk	away from keyboard
ah	a**hole
ai	artificial intelligence
aiamu	and I'm a monkey's uncle
aicmfp	and I claim my five pounds
aight	alright
aiight	alright
aim	AOL Instant Messenger
ain't	am not
aite	alright
aiui	as I understand it
AJAX	asynchronous JavaScript and xml
aka	also known as
alot	a lot

alright	all right
amf	adios motherf**ker
anim8	animate
anon	anonymous
anuda	another
anw	anyways
any1	anyone
anywaz	anyways
aoe	age of empires
ar	are
arnd	around
arse	a**
arsed	bothered
asafp	as soon as f**king possible
asap	as soon as possible

asl	age, sex, location
aslp	age, sex, location, picture
aslr	age sex location race
aslrp	age sex location race picture
atm	at the moment
atop	at time of posting
aup	acceptable use policy
avie	avatar (small picture)
avy	avatar (small picture)
awes	awesome
awk	awkward
awol	absent without leave
ayb	all your base
aybab2u	all your base are belong to us
aybabtu	all your base are belong to us

ayd	are you done
aydy	are you done yet
ayec	at your earliest convenience
aypi?	and your point is?
ayt	are you there
ayte	alright
aytf	are you there f**ker?
azn	asian

B   b |3   13

b'day	birthday
b&	banned
b-cuz	because
b.s.	bullsh*t
b/c	because
b/g	background
b/t	between
b00t	boot
b2b	business to business
b3	be
b4	before
b4n	bye for now
bab	big a** boobs

baf	bring a friend
bah	I don't really care
bai	bye
bak	back
bamf	bad a** mother f**ker
bb	bye bye
bb4n	bye bye for now
bbbj	bare back blow job
bbe	baby
bbiab	be back in a bit
bbiaf	be back in a few
bbiam	be back in a minute
bbiaw	be back in a while
bbl	be back later
bbl8a	be back later

bbml	be back much later
bbq	be back quick
bbs	be back soon
bbw	be back whenever
bbwb	best buddy with boobs
bbwl	be back way later
bbz	babes (or babies)
bc	because
bck	back
bcnu	be seeing you
bcnul8r	be seeing you later
bcuz	because
bday	birthday
beeoch	bit*h
beezy	bit*h

bewb	boob
bewt	boot
bf	boyfriend
bf4e	best friends for ever
bfd	big f**king deal
bfe	bum f**k Egypt
bff	best friend forever
bffae	best friends forever and ever
bffe	best friends forever
bffeae	best friend for ever and ever
bffl	best friends for life
bfg	big f**king gun
bfhd	big fat hairy deal
bfn	bye for now
bft	big f**king tits

bhwu	back home with you
biab	back in a bit
biatch	bit*h
bibi	bye bye
bicbw	but I could be wrong
biw	boss is watching
bizatch	bit*h
bizzle	bit*h
bj	blowjob
bk	back (or Burger King)
bka	better known as
bl	bad luck
bling-bling	jewelry
blj	blowjob
blkm	black male

blog	web log
blogger	web logger
bm	bite me
bmf	be my friend
bmfe	best mates forever
bmha	bite my hairy a**
bn	been
bndm3ovr	bend me over
bnib	brand new in box
bnol	be nice or leave
bofh	bastard operator from hell
bogsatt	bunch of guys sitting around the table
bohic	bend over here it comes
bohica	bend over here it comes again

boi	boy
bol	barking out loud
bout	about
br	bathroom
brb	be right back
brbbrb	be right back bathroom break
brbg2p	be right back got to pee
brbts	be right back taking sh*t
brd	bored
brh	be right here
brt	be right there
bruva	brother
bruz	brothers
bs	bullsh*t
bsod	blue screen of death

bsomn	blowing stuff out my nose
bt	bit torrent
btcn	better than Chuck Norris
btdt	been there done that
btdtgtts	been there done that got the t-shirt
btsoom	beats the sh*t out of me
bttt	been there tried that
btw	by the way
btwn	between
bty	back to you
buhbi	bye bye
burma	be undressed ready my angel
buszay	busy
but6	butt sex
butterface	everything is cute but her face

byes	bye
bykt	but you knew that
byob	bring your own beer
byoc	bring our own computer
bytabm	beat you to a bloody mess
bz	busy
bzzy	busy

C ([©

c 2 c	cam to cam (webcams)
c/t	can't talk
c2	come to
c2c	care to chat?
c4ashg	care for a shag
cancer stick	cigarette
cb	come back
cbf	cant be f**ked
cd9	code 9 (other people nearby)
cex	sex
cexy	sexy
cg	congratulations
chilax	chill and relax in one word

chillin	relaxing
chk	check
chronic	marijuana
chut	p*ssy
cid	consider it done
cig	cigarette
cis	computer information science
cluebie	clueless newbie
cm	call me
cma	cover my a**
cmiiw	correct me if I'm wrong
cml	call me later
cmomc	call me on my cell
cmon	come on
cmplcdd	complicated

cnc	command and conquer
cod	call of duty
code 9	other people near by
cof	crying on the floor
col	crying out loud
comp	computer
coo	cool
cood	could
cos	because
cowboy choker	cigarette
coz	because
cpl	cyber athlete professional league
cpm	cost per 1000 impressions
crazn	crazy Asian

crm	customer relationship management
crp	crap
crs	can't remember sh*t
crunk	combination of crazy and drunk
cs	counter-strike (game)
cs:s	counter-strike: source
csl	can't stop laughing
ct	can't talk
ctc	call the cell
ctf	capture the flag
ctm	chuckle to myself
ctn	can't talk now
ctpc	cant talk parent coming
ctrn	can't talk right now
cu	goodbye

cu46	see you for sex
cubi	can you believe it
cuic	see you in class
cul	see you later
cul83r	see you later
cul8er	see you later
cul8r	see you later
cunt	vagina
cuple	couple
cuwul	catch up with you later
cuz	because
cwot	complete waste of time
cwyl	chat with you later
cya	goodbye
cyb	cyber

cye	close your eyes
cyff	change your font f**ker
cyl	see you later
cyla	see you later, alligator
cylbd	catch you later baby doll
cylor	check your local orthodox rabbi
cym	check your mail
cyu	see you
c|n>k	coffee through nose into keyboard

D   d |) |} |]   c/

d/c	disconnected
d/l	download
d/w	don't worry
d00d	dude
d2	Diablo 2 (video game)
d8	date
da	the
damhik	don't ask me how I know
damhikt	don't ask me how I know this
dat	that
dawg	friend
db4l	drinking buddy for life
dbafwtt	don't be a fool wrap the tool
dbg	don't be gay

dc	don't care
dc'd	disconnected
dcw	doing class work
dd	don't die
ddg	drop dead gorgeous
ddl	direct download
def	definitely
dem	them
der	there
dernoe	I don't know
dewd	dude
dey	they
df	dumb f**k
dfw/m	don't f**k with me
dfwm	don't f**k with me

dgms	don't get me started
dgt	don't go there
dh	dickhead
diaf	die in a fire
dic	do I care?
dil	daughter in law
dilf	dad I'd like to f**k
dillic	do I look like I care?
dillifc	do I look like I f**king care?
dilligad	do I look like I give a damn?
dilligaf	do I look like I give a f**k?
dilligas	do I look like I give a sh*t
din	didn't
din't	didn't
dirl	die in real life

dis	this
dit	details in thread
diy	do it yourself
dju	did you?
dk	don't know
dkdc	don't know, don't care
dl	download
dlf	dropping like flies
dln	don't look now
dm	death match (in a video game)
dmba*	dumb a**
dmy	don't mess yourself
dn	don't know
dnd	do not disturb
dno	don't know

dnrtfa	did not read the f**king article
dnt	don't
doa	dead on arrival
dod	day of defeat (video game)
dogg	friend
doin	doing
don	denial of normal
doncha	don't you
dont	don't
dontcha	don't you
dood	dude
doodz	dudes
dos	denial of service
dotc	dancing on the ceiling
doypov	depends on your point of view

dqydj	don't quit your day job
dt	double team
dta	don't trust anyone
dttm	don't talk to me
dun	don't
dunno	I don't know
dvda	double vaginal, double anal
dw	don't worry
dwt	don't want to talk
dyk	did you know
dynm	do you know me
dyt	don't you think

E e 3

e.g.	example
ecf	error carried forward
eejit	idiot
effing	f**king
eg	evil grin
ehlp	help
eil	explode into laughter
el!t	elite
em	them
emo	emotional
emp	eat my p*ssy
enuf	enough
eob	end of business

eod	end of day
eof	end of file
eom	end of message
eot	end of transmission
eq	Everquest (videogame)
eq2	Everquest 2 (videogame)
ere	here
errythin	everything
esad	eat sh*t and die
esbm	everyone sucks but me
esl	eat sh*t loser
etla	extended three letter acronym
etmda	explain it to my dumb a**
eula	end user license agreement
ev1	everyone

eva	ever
evaa	ever
evercrack	Everquest (addicting video game)
every1	everyone
evry1	every one
exp	experience
eyez	eyes

F f

f u	f**k you
f#cking	f**king
f/o	f**k off
f00k	f**k.
f2f	face to face
f2p	free to play
f4f	female for female
f4m	female for male
fab	fabulous
faggit	faggot
fankle	area between foot and ankle
fap	masturbate
faq	frequently asked question
fawk	f**k

fc	fruit cake
fck	f**k
fcku	f**k you
fcol	for crying out loud
fcuk	f**k
fe	fatal error
fer	for
ff	friendly fire
ffa	free for all
ffcl	falling from chair laughing
ffs	for f**k's sake
fg	f**king gay
fgi	f**king Google it
fgs	for God's sake
fgssu	for God's sake shut up

fgt	faggot
fi	f**k it
fi9	fine
fifo	first in, first out
figmo	f*ck it - got my orders
fiic	f**ked if I care
fiik	f**ked if I know
fio	figure it out
fitb	fill in the blank
fku	f**k you
flamer	angry poster
flames	angry comments
floabt	for lack of a better term
fm	f**k me
fmah	f**k my a** hole

fmao	freezing my a** of
fmb	f**k me bit*h
fmh	f**k me hard
fmn	f**k me now
fmnb	f**k me now bit*h
fmq	f**k me quick
fmr	f**k me running
fmutp	f**k me up the p*ssy
fn	first name
fnar	for no apparent reason
fnci	fancy
fnpr	for no particular reason
fo	f**k off
fo shizzle	for sure
fo sho	for sure

foad	f**k off and die
foaf	friend of a friend
fob	fresh off the boat
fol	farting out loud
folo	follow
fone	phone
foobar	f**ked up beyond all recognition
foocl	falls out of chair laughing
fook	f**k
fotcl	fell off the chair laughing
fotm	flavor of the month
fov	field of view
fo'	for
fp	first post
fpmitap	federal pound me in the a**

fps	first person shooter
frag	kill
fragged	killed
friggin	freaking
frm	from
fs	for sure
fsm	flying spaghetti monster
fsod	frozen screen of death
fst	fast
ft	f**k that
ftf	face to face
ftl	for the lose
ftlog	for the love of god
ftp	file transfer protocol
ftr	for the record

fts	f**k that sh*t
fttp	for the time being
ftw	for the win
fu	f**k you
fubah	f**ked up beyond all hope
fubar	f**ked up beyond all recognition
fubh	f**ked up beyond hope
fktard**	f**king retard
fuctard	f**king retard =
fud	fear, uncertainty, and doubt
fudie	f**k you, die
fugly	f**king ugly
fuk	f**k
fus	f**k yourself
fux	f**k

fuxored	f**ked
fwiw	for what it's worth
fxp	file exchange protocol
fy	f**k you
fya	for your attention
fyad	f**k you and die
fyb	f**k you bit*h
fyc	f**k your couch
fyfi	for your f**king information
fyi	for your information
fyl	for your love

G g 6 9

g	grin
g/f	girlfriend
g/g	got to go
g1	good one
g2g	got to go
g2gp	got to go pee
g2gpp	got to go pee pee
g2h	go to hell
g2p	got to pee
g3y	gay
g4u	good for you
g4y	good for you (or gay)
g8	gate
ga	go ahead

gafi	get away from it
gagf	go and get f**ked
gah	gay a** homo
gai	gay
gaj	get a job
gal	get a life
gamez	illegally obtained games
gaoep	generally accepted office etiquette principles
gbtw	go back to work
gbu	god bless you
gcad	get cancer and die
gcf	google click fraud
gd4u	good for you
gdby	goodbye

gdgd	good good (or good God)
gdiaf	go die in a fire
gdr	grinning, ducking, running
geto	ghetto
gf	girlfriend
gfad	go f**k a duck
gfadh	go f**k a dead horse
gfam	go f**k a monkey
gfas	go f**k a sheep
gfe	girl friend experience
gfe2e	grinning from ear to ear
gfg	good f**king game
gfi	good f**king idea
gfj	good f**king job
gfu	go f**k yourself

gfx	graphics
gfy	good for you
gfym	go f**k your mom
gfys	go f**k yourself
gg	good game
gga	good game all
ggg	go, go, go
ggnore	good game no rematch
ggp	got to go pee
gh	good half
ghey	gay
gigo	garbage in garbage out
gimme	give me
gimmie	give me
gir	Google it retard

gis	Google image search
gj	good job
gjp	good job partner
gjsu	God, just shut up
gjt	good job team
gl	good luck
glln	got laid last night
glty	good luck this year
glu	girl like us
gm	good morning
gmab	give me a break
gmafb	give me a f**king break
gmao	giggling my a** off
gmfao	giggling my f**king a** off
gmod	global moderator

gmta	great minds think alike
gn	good night
gn8	good night
gnight	good night
gnite	good night
gnoc	get naked on cam
gok	god only knows
gokid	got observers keep it decent
goml	get out of my life
gonna	going to
goomh	get out of my head
gork	God only really knows
goya	get off your a**
goyhh	get off your high horse
gp	good point

gpb	got to pee bad
gpwm	good point well made
gr8	great
grats	congratulations
grillz	metal teeth accessories
grl	girl
grog	beer
grrl	girl
grtg	getting ready to go
gsp	get some p*ssy
gsta	gangster
gt	get
gtfa	go the f**k away
gtfbtw	get the f**k back to work
gtfo	get the f**k out

gtfooh	get the f**k out of here
gtfuotb	get the f**k up out this bit*h
gtg	got to go
gtgpp	got to go pee pee
gtgtb	got to go to bed
gth	go to hell
gtha	go the hell away
gthyfah	go to hell you f**king a**hole
gtk	good to know
gtty	good talking to you
gud	good
guru	expert
gw	good work
gwm	gay white male
gwytose	go waste your time on someone else

H   h |-|

h/o	hold on
h2	halo 2 (videogame)
h2o	water
h4x0r	hacker
h4xor	hacker
h4xx0rz	hacker
h8	hate
h8er	hater
h8r	hater
hagn	have a good night
hago	have a good one
hai	hello
hait	hate

hak	here's a kiss
hakas	have a kick a** summer
hammrd	hammered
hav	have
hawt	hot
hax	hacks
hax0r	hacker
hax0red	hacked
hax0rz	hackers
haxer	hacker
haxor	hacker
haxoring	hacking
haxxor	hacker
hayd	how are you doing
hb	hurry back

hbd	happy birthday
hbu	how about you
hby	how about you
hc	how come
hcihy	how can I help you
hdop	help delete online predators
heh	ha ha
hella	very
heyy	hello
hf	have fun
hfn	hell f**king no
hfs	holy f**king sh*t!
hhiadb	holy hole in a donut batman
hhok	ha ha only kidding
hi2u	hello

hi2u2	hello to you too
hj	hand job
hl	half-life (video game)
hl2	half-life 2 (video game)
hla	hot lesbian action
hldn	hold on
hll	hell
hmfic	head mother f**ker in charge
hmw	homework
hng	horny net geek
hnic	head nigga in charge
ho	hold on
hoas	hang on a second
homey	friend
homie	good friend

hoopty	broke down automobile
hott	hot
howdey	hello
hpb	high ping bastard
hpybdy	happy birthday
hre	here
hru	how are you
hrud	how are you doing
hs	headshot
hss	horse sh*t and splinters
hswm	have sex with me
htc	hit the cell
htf	how the f**k
hth	hope that helps
http	hyper text transfer protocol

hud	heads up display
huggle	hug and cuddle
hugz	hugs
hw	homework
hw?	how?
hwg	here we go
hwga	here we go again
hwmbo	he who must be obeyed
hyg	here you go

I I ! 1 |

I C	I see
i8	alright
iab	I am bored
iag	it's all good
iah	I am horny
ianacl	I am not a copyright lawyer
ianal	I am not a lawyer
ianalb	I am not a lawyer, but..
ianars	I am not a rocket scientist
iaw	in another window
iawtc	I agree with this comment
iawtp	I agree with this post
ib	I'm back
ibcd	idiot between chair and desk

ibs	internet bit*h slap
ibtl	in before the lock
ic	I see
icbiwoop	I chuckled, but it was out of pity.
icgup	I can give you pleasure
icp	insane clown posse (band)
ictrn	I can't talk right now
icudk	in case you didn't know
icup	I see you pee
icw	I care why?
icydk	in case you didn't know
icydn	in case you didn't know
id10t	idiot
idc	I don't care

idec	I don't even care
idek	I don't even know
idfc	I don't f**king care
idfk	I don't f**king know
idgac	I don't give a crap
idjit	idiot
idk	I don't know
idkh	I don't know how
idkh2s	I don't know how to spell
idkw	I don't know why
idkwurta	I don't know what you're talking about.
idly	I don't like you
idonno	I do not know
idr	I don't remember

idts	I don't think so
idunno	I do not know
iduwym	I don't understand what you mean.
idwt	I don't want to
iebkac	issue exists between keyboard and chair
igahp	I've got a huge penis
igalboc	I've got a lovely bunch of coconuts
ight	alright
igtgt	I've got to go tinkle
igtkya	I'm going to kick your a**
ih2gp	I have to go pee
ih2p	I'll have to pass
ih8mls	I hate my little sister
ih8p	I hate parents

ih8u	I hate you
ihac	I have a customer
ihnfc	I have no f**king clue
ihni	I have no idea
ihtfp	I hate this f**king place
ihtp	I have to poop
ihu	I hate you
ihy	I hate you
iight	alright
iirc	if I recall correctly
iistgtbtipi	if it sounds too good to be true it probably is
iiuc	if I understand correctly
ijf	I just farted
ijgl	I just got laid

ijit	idiot
ijpmp	I just peed my pants
ik	I know
ikwum	I know what you meant
ikwym	I know what you mean
ilbcnu	I'll be seeing you
ilk2fku	I would like to f**k you
ilotibinlirl	I'm laughing on the internet, but I'm not laughing in real life
ilu	I love you
ilusm	I love you so much
iluvya	I love you
iluwamh	I love you with all my heart
ily	I love you
ily2	I love you too

ilym	I love you more
ilysfm	I love you so f**king much
im	instant message
im'd	instant messaged
ima	I am a
imao	in my arrogant opinion
imcdo	in my conceited dogmatic opinion
imed	instant messaged
imfao	in my f**king arrogant opinion
imh	I am here
imhbco	in my humble but correct opinion
imhe	in my humble experience
imho	in my humble opinion
imnerho	in my not even remotely humble opinion

imnsho	in my not so humble opinion
imo	in my opinion
impov	in my point of view
imvho	in my very humble opinion
imwtk	inquiring minds want to know
indie	independent
inet	internet
inho	in my honest opinion
inmp	it's not my problem
ino	I know
interweb	internet
inttwmf	I am not typing this with my fingers
ioh	I'm out of here
iokiya	it's ok if you are

iono	I don't know
iow	in other words
ip	internet protocol
irc	internet relay chat
irhtgttbr	I really have to go to the bathroom
irl	in real life
irt	in reply to
isg	I speak geek
isianmtu	I swear I am not making this up
iso	in search of
isp	internet service provider
istr	I seem to remember
itk	in the know
itt	in this thread

ityltk	I thought you'd like to know
itz	it's
iucmd	if you catch my drift
iukwim	if you know what I mean
iuno	i dunno
ive	I have
iw2mu	I want to meet you
iwfusb	I want to f**k you so bad
iwhi	I would hit it
iws	I want sex
iwu	I want you
iydmma	if you don't mind me asking
iykwim	if you know what I mean
iym	I am your man
iz	is

J j

j/c	just curious
j/k	just kidding
j/o	jack off
j/p	just playing
j/w	just wondering
j00	you
j00r	your
j4f	just for fun
j4u	just for you
jas	just a second
jc	just curious
jcam	just checking away message
jcath	just chilling at the house
jdfi	just f**king do it

jfc	Jesus f**king Christ
jfdi	just f**king do it!
jfg	just for giggles
jfgi	just f**king Google it
jfk	just f**king kidding
jfwy	just f**king with you
jgiyn	just Google it you newbie
jhm	just hold me
jic	just in case
jit	just in time
jj	just joking
jj/k	just joking
jk	just kidding
jka	just kidding around
jma	just messing around

jmo	just my opinion
jms	just making sure
jom	just one minute
joo	you
jooc	just out of curiosity
joor	your
jp	just playing
jst	just
jsuk	just so you know
jsut	just
jtol	just thinking out loud
jus	just
juzt	just
jw	just wondering
jyfihp	jam your finger in her p*ssy

K k

k3wl	cool
kafn	kill all f**king newbies
kaw	kick a** work
kb	kilobyte
kewl	cool
khitbash	kick her in the box and shove her
kicks	sneakers
kinda	kind of
kir	kid in room
kis	keep it simple
kit	keep in touch
kitfo	knock it the f**k off
kiwf	kill it with fire
kk	ok

kl	cool
kma	kiss my a**
kmfa	kiss my f**king a**
knackered	drunk
knewb	new player
kno	know
knw	know
kol	kiss on lips
kool	cool
kotc	kiss on the cheek
kotor	knights of the old republic
kots	keep on talking sh*t
ks	kill steal
kthanxbi	okay, thanks. bye.
kthnxbai	okay, thanks, bye

kthnxbye	okay, thanks, bye
kthx	ok, thank you
kthxbai	ok thanks bye
kthxbi	ok, thank you, goodbye
kthxbye	ok, thank you, goodbye
kthxbye	ok, thank you, goodbye
kuhl	cool
kuwl	cool
kwim	know what I mean?
kwit	quit
kwl	cool
kwtsds	kiss where the sun don't shine
kyfc	keep your fingers crossed
kys	kill yourself

L l | 1

l2p	learn to play
l2r	learn to read
l337	elite
l33t	elite
l4m3rz	lamers
l8	late
l84skool	late for school
l8a	later
l8er	later
l8r	see you later
l8s	later
l8t	later
l8ter	later
l8tr	later

lak	love and kisses
lalol	lots and lots of laughs
lam	leave a message
lamf	like a mother f**ker
lat	laugh at that
lates	later
latn	laugh at the newbies
latwttb	laughing all the way to the bank
lau	laugh at you
lawl	southern laughing out loud
lawlz	southern laughing out loud
lbr	little boy's room
lee7	elite
leet	elite
leik	like

lemme	let me
lesbo	lesbian
less than three	love (<3 looks like a heart)
lez	lesbian
lf1m	looking for one more
lfg	looking for group
lfm	looking for mate
lfr	laughing for real
lgb	lesbian/gay/bisexual
lgbnaf	lets get butt naked and f**k
lgf	little green footballs (website)
lgs	let's go shopping
liek	like
lifo	last in first out
ligaff	like I give a flying f**k

ligafs	like I give a flying sh*t
ligas	like I give a sh*t
lik	like
lil	little
limh	laugh in my head
lirl	laughing in real life
liyf	laughing in your face
lj	live journal (website)
lk	like
llap	live long and prosper
llol	literally laughing out loud
lm4aq	let's meet for a quickie.
lma	leave me alone
lmamf	leave me alone mother f**ker
lmao	laughing my a** off

lmaonade	laughing my a** off
lmaorof	laughing my a** off rolling on the floor
lmaorotf	laughing my a** off rolling on the floor
lmaoxh	laughing my a** off extremely hard
lmbfwao	laughing my big fat white a** off
lmbo	laughing my butt off
lmclao	laughing my cute little a** off
lmfao	laughing my f**king a** off
lmffo	laughing my f**king face off
lmfho	laughing my f**king head off
lmfpo	laughing my f**king p*ssy off
lmhao	laughing my hairy a** off
lmho	laughing my heiny off
lmirl	let's meet in real life

lmk	let me know
lmmfao	laughing my mother f**king a** off
lmo	leave me one
lmoao	laughing my other a** off
lmpo	laughing my panties off
lmso	laughing my socks off
lmtfa	leave me the f**k alone
lmto	laughing my tits off
ln	last name
lobfl	laugh out bloody f**king loud
lol	laughing out loud
lol'd	laughed out loud
lolcity	the whole city laughs out loud
lold	laughed out loud
lolees	laugh out loud

lolin	laughing out loud
lollercaust	an extreme event of hilarity
lollercoaster	laugh out loud
lollerskates	laughing out loud
lololz	laugh out loud
lolpimp	laughing out loud peeing in my pants
lolrotf	laughing out loud rolling on the floor
lols	laugh out loud
lolz	laugh out loud
loti	laughing on the inside
loxen	laughing out loud
loxxen	laughing out loud
lpb	low ping bastard
lpms	life pretty much sucks

lshismp	laughed so hard I sh*t my pants
lsr	loser
ltip	laughing until I puke
ltns	long time no see
ltnsoh	long time no see or hear
ltp	lay the pipe
ltr	later
ltw	lead the way
lu2	love you too
lu4l	love you for life
lub	laugh under breath
lug	lesbian until graduation
lulab	love you like a brother
lulas	love you like a sister
lurker	one who reads but doesn't reply

luser	user who is a loser
luv	love
lv	love
lvl	level
lvya	love you
ly	love you
lyk	like
lyk3	like
lyke	like
lyl	love you lots
lylab	love you like a brother
lylafklc	love you like a fat kid loves cake
lylas	I love you like a sister
lylno	love you like no other
lyls	love you lots

lymi	love you mean it
lysm	love you so much
lyt	love you too
lzr	loser

M m /\/\

m$	Microsoft
m.o	make out
m/b	maybe
m/f	male or female
m2	me too
m473s	mates (friends)
m473z	mates (friends)
m4f	male for female
m4m	male for male
m8	mate (friend)
mah	my
mao	my a** off
marvy	marvelous
mayb	maybe

mbf	my best friend
mcs	my computer sucks
me2	me too
meatcurtain	woman's private parts
meatspace	the real world
mego	my eyes glaze over
meh	whatever
mf	motherf**ker
mfa	mother f**king a**hole
mfao	my f**king a** off
mfg	merge from current
mhh	my head hurts
mhm	yes
mho	my humble opinion
mia	missing in action

mic	microphone
milf	mom I'd like to f**k
mir	mom in room
mirl	meet in real life
misc.	miscellaneous
miself	myself
miwnlf	mom I would not like to f**k.
mk	mmm ok
mlod	mega laugh out loud of doom
mmw	make me wet
mngmt	management
mnm	Eminem (singer)
mobo	motherboard
mod	moderator or modification
mofo	mother f**ker

mohaa	medal of honor allied assault
mompl	moment please
moobs	man boobs
mor	more
morf	male or female
mos	mom over shoulder
moss	member of same sex
motarded	more retarded
motd	message of the day
motos	member of the opposite sex
mpih	my penis is hard
mpty	more power to you
ms	Microsoft
msg	message
msh	me so horny

msibo	my side is busting open
msm	main stream media
mtf	more to follow
musm	miss you so much
mutha	mother
mwf	married white female
myke	man-dyke
myob	mind your own business
mypl	my young pad wan learner

N n /\/

mmorpg	massively multiplayer online role playing game
n/a	not applicable (not available)
n/m	never mind
n00b	newbie
n00bs	newbies
n00s	news
n1	nice one
n2	into
n2g	not too good
n2m	not too much
n2mh	not too much here
n2mu	not too much, you?
na	not applicable

naww	no
nbd	no big deal
ndit	no details in thread
ne	any
ne1	anyone
neday	any day
nemore	anymore
nething	anything
neva	never
nevah	never
neway	anyway
neways	anyways
newayz	anyways
newb	someone who is new
newbie	new player

nfbsk	not for British school kids
nfc	no f**king clue
nfi	no f**king idea
nfs	not for sale
nft	no further text
nfw	no f**king way
ng	nice game
nh	nice hand
ni	no idea
nifoc	naked in front of computer
nifok	naked in front of keyboard
nigysob	now I've got you son of a bit*h
nimby	not in my backyard
nin	no it's not
nip	nothing in particular

nizzle	African American
nj	nice job
nk	no kidding
nld	nice lay down
nm	not much
nm u	not much, you
nmh	not much here
nmhau	nothing much how about you
nmhm	nothing much here, man
nmhu	nothing much here, you?
nmhwby	nothing much here what about you
nmjc	not much, just chilling
nmjch	nothing much just chilling
nmjfa	nothing much, just f**king around

nmnhnlm	no money, no honey, nobody loves me
nmu	nothing much, you
nn	good night
nolm	no one loves me
noob	someone who is new
noobie	new person
nooblet	new player
noobz0r	newbie
nookie	sex
nop	normal operating procedure
norwich	knickers off ready when I come home
nowai	no way
nowin	knowing
noyb	none of your business

np	no problem
npa	not paying attention
nph	no problem here
npi	no pun intended
npnt	no picture, no talk
nr	no reserve
nr4u	not right for you
nrg	energy
nrn	no response necessary
ns	nice
nsa	no strings attached
nsfw	not safe for work
nss	no sh*t Sherlock
nstaafl	no such thing as a free lunch
nt	nice try

ntb	not to bad
ntm	not to much
ntt	need to talk
nttiawwt	not that there is anything wrong with that.
ntxt	no text
nty	no thank you
nu	new
nufin	nothing
nvm	never mind
nw	no way
nws	not work safe
ny1	anyone

O o 0 p ()

o rly	oh really
o rly?	oh really?
oar	on a roll
obtw	oh, by the way
obv	obviously
ofc	of course
ofcol	oh for crying out loud
oftn	often
ogw	oh guess what
oh noes	oh no
ohic	oh I see
oic	oh, I see
oj	orange juice
oll	online love

omfg	oh my f**king God
omfwtg	oh my f**k what the God?
omg	oh my God
omgsh	oh my gosh
omgwtf	on my God, what the f**k
omgwtfbbq	oh my God, what the f**k
omgwtfhax	oh my God what the f**k, hacks
omgwtfnipples	oh my God, what the f**k
omgz	oh my God
omgzors	oh my God
omhg	oh my hell God
ommfg	oh my mother f**king God
omw	on my way
omy	oh my
ooc	out of character

oom	out of mana (or money)
ooo	out of the office
op	operator
orly	oh really?
os	operating system
ot	off topic
otfcu	on the floor cracking up
otflmao	on the floor laughing my a** off
otflmfao	on the floor laughing my f**king a** off
otflol	on the floor laughing out loud
otfp	on the f**king phone
otl	out to lunch
otoh	on the other hand
otp	on the phone

otw	on the way
owned	made to look bad
ownt	made to look bad
ownz	owns
ownzer	one who makes others look bad
oyfe	open your f**king eyes

P p

p-nis	penis
p.o.s	parent over shoulder
p0wn	(own) make to look bad
p2p	peer to peer
p3n0r	penis
p911	parent emergency (parent near)
pae	pimping aint easy
pasii	put a sock in it
paw	parents are watching
pb	peanut butter
pb&j	peanut butter and jelly
pbj	peanut butter and jelly
pbly	probably
pcbd	page cannot be displayed

pcrs	parents can read slang
pda	public display of affection
pdq	pretty damn quick
pearoast	repost
pebcak	problem exists between chair and keyboard
pebkac	problem exists between keyboard and chair
pebmac	problem exist between monitor and chair
peeps	people
pen0r	penis
pen15	penis
pezzas	parents
pfo	please f**k off
pfos	parental figure over shoulder

pfy	pimply faced youth
pg	page
ph33r	fear
ph34r	fear
phag	fag
phat	pretty hot and tasty
phear	fear
phq	f**k you
phreak	freak
phreaker	phone hacker
phuck	f**k
phucker	f**ker
phun	fun
phux	f**k
pic	picture

pics	pictures
pihb	pee in his/her butt
pima	pain in my a**
pimfa	pain in my f**king a**
pimha	pain in my hairy a**
pimpl	pissing in my pants laughing
pino	Filipino
pir	parents in room
pita	pain in the a**
pix	pictures
pl0x	please
ple's	please
pleez	please
plocks	please
plomb	parents looking over my back

ploms	parent looking over my shoulder
plos	parents looking over shoulder
plox	please
pls	please
plx	please/thanks
plz	please
plzkthx	please? ok, thank you
plzthx	please? thanks
pmfji	pardon me for jumping in
pmg	oh my god
pmitap	pound me in the a** prison
pml	pissing myself laughing
pmp	pissing my pants
pmpl	piss my pants laughing
pmsl	piss my self laughing

po	piss off
po po	police
po'd	pissed off
poets	piss off early, tomorrow's Saturday
poms	parent over my shoulder
poo	poop
poontang	female genitalia
popo	police
poq	piss off quick
pos	parent over shoulder
pov	point of view
pow	prisoner of war
pp	pee pee
ppl	people

ppls	people
pplz	people
ppor	post proof or recant
ppppppp	prior proper planning prevents piss poor performance
pr0	professional
pr0n	porn
pro	professional
prolly	probably
pron	porn
prp	please reply
prv	private
prvrt	pervert
prw	parents are watching
psbms	parent standing by my side

ptbb	pass the barf bag
pvp	player versus player
pw	parent watching / password
pwb	p*ssy whipped bit*h
pwn	made to look bad
pwn3d	owned
pwnage	ownage
pwnd	owned
pwned	made to look bad
pwnt	owned
pwnz	owns
pxr	punk rocker
pydim	put your d*ck in me

Q q

qed	end of proof
qfe	quoted for emphasis
qft	quoted for truth
ql	cool
qool	cool
qoolz	cool
qotd	quote of the day
qotsa	queens of the stone age (band)
qpwd	quit posting while drunk
qq	crying eyes
qt	cutie

R r

r0x0rz	rocks
r8	rate
rawks	rocks
rawr	roar
re	reply
rehi	hello again
reefer	marijuana
refl	rolling on the floor laughing
rehi	hello again
rents	parents
rentz	parents
rep	to represent
reppin	representing
rff	really f**king funny

rflmao	rolling on floor laughing my a** off
rgr	roger
rihad	rot in hell and die
rino	republican in name only
rite	right
rl	real life
rlbf	real life boy friend
rlf	real life friend
rlg	really loud giggle
rlgf	real life girl friend
rln	real life name
rly	really
rnt	aren't
ro	rock out
rodger	affirmative

roffle	rolling on the floor laughing
rofflecake	rolling on the floor laughing
roffles	rolling on floor laughing
rofl	rolling on the floor laughing
roflcopter	rolling on the floor laughing
roflmao	rolling on floor laughing my a** off
roflmfao	rolling on the floor laughing my f**king a** off
roflmbo	rolling on floor laughing my butt off
roflol	rolling on floor laughing out loud
rofpml	rolling on the floor pissing myself laughing
rofwl	rolling on the floor while laughing
roger	affirmative
rogl	rolling on ground laughing
roj	affirmative

rol	rolling over laughing
rolmao	rolling over laughing my a** off
roofles	rolling on the floor laughing
rotf	rolling on the floor
rotfl	rolling on the floor laughing
rotflmao	rolling on the floor laughing my a** off
rotflmaostc	rolling on the floor laughing my a** off scaring the cat
rotflol	rolling on the floor laughing out loud
rotg	rolling on the ground
rowyco	rock out with your co*k out
roxorz	rocks
rpg	role playing game
rr	rest room
rrb	restroom break

rsn	real soon now
rta	read the article
rtbq	read the blinking question
rtfa	read the f**king article
rtffp	read the f**king front page
rtfm	read the f**king manual
rtfmfm	read the f**king manual f**king moron
rtfmm	read the f**king manual moron
rtfp	read the f**king post
rtfq	read the f**king question
rtfu	ready the f**k up
rtl	report the loss
rtm	read the manual
rtry	retry

rts	real time strategy
ru	are you
rua	are you alone
rumf?	are you male or female?
ruok	are you ok?
rut	are you there
rwb	rich white bit*h
ryte	right

S s 5 $ Z

s	smile
s'pose	suppose
s.i.n.g.l.e	stay intoxicated nightly, get laid everyday (from Jeff Foxworthy)
s.i.t.	stay in touch
s/b	should be
s/n	screen name
s2bu	sucks to be you
s2r	send to receive
sagn	spelling and grammar Nazi
scnr	sorry, I couldn't resist
scurred	scared
sd	suck d*ck
sdf^	shut the f**k up

secks	sex
secksea	sexy
sed	said
seo	search engine optimization
serp	search engine results page
sexe	sexy
sexi	sexy
sexilicious	very sexy
sez	says
sfm	so f**king much
sfsg	so far so good
sfu	shut the f**k up
sfw	safe for work
sgb	straight/gay/bisexual
sh	sh*t happens

shd	should
shiznat	sh*t
shiznit	sh*t
shizzle	sh*t
shmily	see how much I love you
sho'nuff	sure enough
shrn	so hot right now
sht	sh*t
shud	should
shyt	sh*t
sibir	sibling in room
sicl	sitting in chair laughing
sif	as if
sifn't	as if not
sig	signature

siggy	signature
simclmao	sitting in my chair laughing my a** off
sk	spawn kill (gaming term)
sk8	skate
sk8er	skater
sk8r	skater
sk8ter	skater
sked	schedule
skeet	ejaculate
skewl	school
skillz	skills
skool	school
sktr	skater
sleepn	sleeping

slf	sexy little f**k
slore	slutty whore
slt	something like that
smc	suck my co*k
smd	suck my d*ck
smdb	suck my d*ck bit*h
smdvq	suck my d*ck quickly
smfd	suck my f**king d*ck
smh	shaking my head
smt	suck my tits
sn	screen name
snafu	situation normal all f**ked up
snafubar	situation normal all f**ked up beyond all recognition
snog	kiss (british)

soa	service oriented architecture
soab	son of a bit*h
soad	system of a down
sob	son of a bit*h
soe	service oriented enterprise
sof	smile on face
soi	service oriented infrastructure
sok	it's ok
sol	sh*t out of luck
som'm	something
som1	someone
soobs	saggy boobs
sorta	sort of
sos	same old sh*t (or spouse over shoulder)

sosdd	same old sh*t, different day
sosg	spouse over shoulder gone
sot	suck on this
soz	sorry
sploits	exploits
sploitz	exploits
srly	seriously (or surely)
sroucks	that's cool, but it still sucks
srry	sorry
srsly	seriously
sry	sorry
ss4l	smoking sister for life
ssdd	same sh*t, different day
ssdp	same sh*t different pile
ssia	subject says it all

ssob	stupid sons of bit*hes
st1	stoned
stbx	soon to be ex
steamloller	laughing a lot
stfd	sit the f**k down
stfm	search the f**king manual
stfng	search the f**king news group
stfu	shut the f**k up
stfua	shut the f**k up already
stfuppercut	shut the f**k up
stfuyb	shut the f**k up you bit*h
stfw	search the f**king web
sth	something
sthu	shut the hell up
stoopid	stupid

str8	straight
su	shut up
suagooml	shut up and get out of my life
suk	suck
sukz	sucks
sul	see you later
sumtin	something
sup	what's up
susfu	situation unchanged, still f**ked up
sut	see you tomorrow
sux	sucks
sux0rz	sucks
sux2bu	sucks to be you
suxor	sucks
suxors	sucks

suxorz	sucks
suxx	sucks
suxxor	sucks
swafk	sealed with a friendly kiss
swak	sealed with a kiss
swalk	sealed with a loving kiss
swmbo	she who must be obeyed
swt	sweet
sxc	sexy
sxy	sexy
sydim	stick your d*ck in me
syl	see you later
syrs	see you real soon
syt	see you there

T t 7 +

t#3	the
tftfy	there, fixed that for you
t2m	talk to me
t2ul	talk to you later
t3h	the
ta	thanks again
tanstaafl	there aint no such thing as a free lunch
tard	retard
tat	that (or tattoo)
tat2	tattoo
taw	teachers are watching
tba	to be announced
tbc	to be continued

tbd	to be decided
tbh	to be honest
tbnt	thanks but no thanks
tbp	the pirate bay (website)
tbqh	to be quite honest
tc	take care
tcp	transmission control protocol
tdtm	talk dirty to me
te	team effort
teh	the
terd	sh*t
tfa	the f**king article
tfbundy	totally f**ked but unfortunately not dead yet
tff	that's f**king funny

tffw	too funny for words
tfic	tongue firmly in cheek
tfu	that's f**ked up
tgfitw	the greatest fans in the world
tgft	thank god for that
tghig	thank god husband is gone
tgif	thank God it's Friday
tgsttttptct	thank god someone took the time to put this crap together
tgtbt	too good to be true
tha	the
thankx	thank you
thanq	thank you
thanx	thank you
thatz	that's

thnx	thanks
tho	though
thr	there
tht	that
thwdi	that's how we do it
thx	thank you
thz	thank you
tia	thanks in advance
tiafayh	thanks in advance for all your help
tiai	take it all in
tis	is
tjb	that's just boring
tk	team kill
tks	thanks
tku	thank you

tl	tough luck
tl; dr	to long; didn't read
tla	three letter acronym
tldr	too long, didn't read
tlgo	the list goes on
tmaai	tell me all about it
tmai	tell me about it
tmi	too much information
tmr	tomorrow
tmr@ia	the monkeys are at it again
tn1	trust no-one
tnx	thanks
tomm	tomorrow
tos	terms of service
totp	talking on the phone

tpiwwp	this post is worthless without pictures
tps	test procedure specification
tptb	the powers that be
trani	trans-sexual
troll	person who causes trouble on forums
ts	talking sh*t
tsff	that's so f**king funny
tsig	that site is gay
tswc	tell someone who cares
tt4n	ta ta for now
ttbomk	to the best of my knowledge
ttfn	ta ta for now
ttihlic	try to imagine how little I care

ttiuwop	this thread is useless without pics
ttly	totally
ttms	talking to myself
ttrf	that's the rules, f**ker
ttth	talk to the hand
ttul	talk to you later
ttyl	talk to you later
ttys	talk to you soon
ttyt	talk to you tomorrow
ttytt	to tell you the truth
tuh	to
tw	teacher watching
twajs	that was a joke, son.
twfaf	that's what friends are for

twoh	typing with one hand
tx	thanks
txt	text
ty	thank you
tyclo	turn your caps lock off
tyclos	turn your caps lock off, stupid
tyfi	thank you for invite
typ	thank you partner
typo	typing mistake
tyt	take your time
tyty	thank you thank you
tyvm	thank you very much

U u

u'd	you would
u'll	you will
u'v	you have
u've	you've
u/l	upload
u2	you too
u2u	up to you
u4i	up for it
ua	user agreement
ub3r	super
uber	super (from German)
ufia	unsolicited finger in the anus
ufic	unsolicited finger in chili

ufmf	you funny mother f**ker
ugtr	you got that right
uhab	you have a blog
uhems	you hardly ever make sense
ui	user interface
ul	unlucky
umfriend	sexual partner (this is my…ummm…friend)
un2bo	you need to back off
upia	unsolicited pencil in anus
ur	your
ura	you are a
uradrk	you're a dork
urs	yours
ursg	you are so gay

urtb	you are the best
urtbitw	you are the best in the world!
urtw	you are the worst
uryyfm	you are too wise for me
usuk	you suck
usux	you suck
ut	unreal tournament (game)
uve	you've
uya	up your a**
uyab	up your a** bit*h

V v V

vb	visual basic
vbeg	very big evil grin
vbg	very big grin
vff	very f**king funny
vfm	value for money
voip	voice over IP
vry	very
vwd	very well done
vweg	very wicked evil grin
vzit	visit

W w \W/

w.e.	whatever
w/	with
w/e	whatever
w/eva	whatever
w/o	with out
w/out	without
w/u	with you
w00t	woohoo
w012d	word
w2g	way to go
w8	wait
w?	what?
wab	what a bit*h
wad	without a doubt

wad ^	what's up?
wadr	with all due respect
waf	weird as f**k
wafl	what a f**king loser
wafn	what a f**king noob
wai	what an idiot
walstib	what a long strange trip it's been
wan2tlk	want to talk
wana	want to
wanafuk	wanna f**k
wanker	masterbater
wanna	want to
warez	illegally obtained software
wassup	what's up?
wasup	what's up

was^	what's up
wat	what
wat's^	what's up
watev	whatever
wateva	whatever
watevr	whatever
wats	what is
wats ^	what is up
wats^	what is up?
watz ^	what is up
wauo	why are you ooing
waw	what a whore
way?	what about you?
wayd	what are you doing
wayg?	where are you going?

waysw	why are you so weird
waz	was
waz ^	what's up
wazz	what's
wazza	what's up
waz^	what's up?
wb	welcome back
wbagnfarb	would be a good name for a rock band
wbp	welcome back partner
wbs	write back soon
wc	who cares
wc3	WarCraft 3 (videogame)
wcw	webcam whore (or wrestling league)
wd	well done

wdum	what do you mean
wduwta	what do you want to talk about
wdwgw?	where did we go wrong?
wdyw	what do you want
weg	wicked evil grin
wen	when
werkz	works
wev	whatever
wevr	whatever
wg	wicked grin
wgaf	who gives a f**k?
wgasa	who gives a sh*t anyway?
wgph2	want to go play halo 2?
whaletail	thong
whatev	whatever

whats ^	what's up
what^	what is up?
whf	want to have fun?
whodi	friend
whr	where
wht	what
whteva	whatever
whtvr	whatever
wht^	what up
widout	without
wif	with
wio	without
wit	with
wit?	who is this?
witcha	with you

wiv	with
wl	will
wn	when
wochit	watch it
woft	waste of f**king time
wogge	what on god's green earth?
wogs	waste of good sperm
wombat	waste of money, brains, and time
woot	woohoo
wot	what
wowzers	wow
woz	was
wow	World of Warcraft (videogame)
wrk	work
wrt	with regard to

wru	where are you
wrud	what are you doing
wsb	want to cyber?
wtb	want to buy
wtbd	what's the big deal
wtbh	what the bloody hell
wtc	what the crap (or world trade center)
wtd	what the deuce
wtf	what the f**k
wtfaud	what the f**k are you doing?
wtfay	who the f**k are you?
wtfduw	what the f**k do you want?
wtfh	what the f**king hell
wtfigo	what the f**k is going on
wtfiyp	what the f**k is your problem

wtfm	what the f**k, mate?
wtfrud	what the f**k are you doing?
wtfwjd	what the f**k would Jesus do
wtg	way to go
wtgp	want to go private
wth	what the heck
wtharud	what the heck are you doing?
wtiiot	what time is it over there?
wtityb	whatever, tell it to your blog
wts	want to sell
wtt	want to trade
wtva	whatever
wtvr	whatever
wu	what's up?
wubu2	what you been up to

wud	would
wuny	wait until next year
wussup	what is up?
wut	what
wuteva	whatever
wuts	what is
wuu2	what you up too
wuwt	what's up with that
wuwu	what up with you
wuz	was
wwdhd	what would David Hasselhoff do?
wwjd	what would Jesus do?
www	world wide web
wy	why?
wyas	wow you are stupid

wyltk	wouldn't you like to know
wylym	watch your language young man
wys	wow you're stupid
wysiayg	what you see is all you get
wysiwyg	what you see is what you get
wywh	wish you were here
wywo	while you were out
w\e	whatever

X x ><

x treme	extreme
xd	extreme droll
xing	crossing
xit	exit
xlnt	excellent
xmas	Christmas
xoac	Christ on a crutch
xor	hacker
xoxo	hugs and kisses
xplaned	explained
xs	excess
xtreme	extreme
xyz	examine your zipper

Y y

y w	you're welcome
y/o	years old
y00	you
ya	yeah
yaai	you are an idiot
yaf	you're a fag
yafi	you're a f**king idiot
yag	you are gay
yall	you all
yapa	yet another pointless acronym
yasfg	you are so f**king gay
yaw	you are welcome
ydpos	you dumb piece of sh*t
yea	yeah

yermom	your mother
yew	you
ygm	you got mail
ygpm	you've got a private message
ygtbkm	you got to be kidding me
ygtsr	you got that sh*t right
yhbt	you've been trolled
yhl	you have lost
yhpm	you have a private message
yid	yes, I do
yim	Yahoo Instant Messenger
ykn	you know nothing
ylb	you little bit*h
ym	your mom
ymbkm	you must be kidding me

ymgtc	your mom goes to college
ymmv	your mileage may vary
yng	young
ynk	you never know
yomank	you owe me a new keyboard
yooh	you
yor	your
youngin	young person
ypmo	you piss me off
yrms	you rock my socks
ys	you suck
ysati	you suck at the internet
ysitm	your shirt is too small
yt	you there?
ytf	why the f**k

ytm	you tell me
ytmnd	you're the man now, dog
yuo	you
yvw	you're very welcome
yw	you're welcome
ywia	you're welcome in advance
yws	you want sex

Z z 2

zh	zero hour
zig	cigarette
zomg	oh my god
zoot	woo hoo
zot	zero tolerance
zup	what's up?

Common Internet Slang Trends

The internet language is constantly evolving and new slang is being created every day. Eventually you're bound to encounter some slang that isn't listed in this book, but don't worry! Just follow these tips and you'll be able to make sense almost any online lingo. You might even be able to create some new words of your own!

1. Numbers or symbols replace words that they might sound like or resemble. (@ might be at, 8 could be –ate, 3 could be an E, or |3 instead of a B.

2. Letters may be substituted for others that sound like them. Examples include ph replacing f, x replacing s, or x replacing c or k.

3. Vowels may be left out. It's very common in slang to write words like "tomorrow" as "tmrrw".

4. Mistakes aren't corrected. Words like teh are left as they are, spacing errors "lik ethis" are very common.

5. Suffixes may be added to words. Some common suffixes include –xor -zor and bie as in roxor, ownzor, and newbie.

6. Spelling, grammar, and punctuation aren't paid particular attention.

The Slang Debate

I've often been asked by newspapers for my take on internet slang. Many journalists are quick to blame slang for the educational downfall of America, yet others praise it for bringing out the creativity of our youth.

On one hand, slang is perverting the English language. The writing skills of America's young people are on a rapid decline and literacy rates are dropping across the country, but is it slang's fault?

On the other hand, the character limits and small keyboards of today's wireless devices certainly inspire our youth to be creative. While they may not be putting their minds to the most productive uses, it's hard to discourage creativity wherever it may rear up.

The way I look at it, the English language is evolving- it has to. If it didn't evolve we'd still be saying words like "thine, thou, and hast." To illustrate how far English has already evolved, my word processor underlined some of those words.

While I personally don't agree with the way the language is evolving, I do feel it's important that we let it evolve. Innovation is important in all areas of life. Today's teens will shape the future of the English language, it's our job to encourage them and guide them along the way.

Other Resources

For a constantly updated list of slang words, please visit this book's website at **www.noslang.com**

There you'll find a more updated slang dictionary, interactive translator, articles about slang, and any book updates or errata.

External Resources

In addition to noslang.com, there are several other quality websites where information about internet slang can be found. Here are a few good sites that I'm not affiliated with:

NetLingo.com – NetLingo contains just about any type of acronym that isn't listed on NoSlang.com. It specializes in business and technical jargon.

Abbreviationz.com – Abbreviationz contains abbreviations in a large number of categories including: Business, Computing, Internet, Chat, Slang, Government, Medical, Science, Military and more.

TheParentsEdge.com – The Parents Edge is a great resource for parents looking for further ways to both protect and educate their kids online.

Ryan's Tips for Parents

Let's face it, many parents don't understand technology as well as their kids do. You read the news articles, you know what dangers are lurking out there on the internet. Here's some tips that will help you keep your kids safe on the net.

1. Talk to your kids. It may sound simple, but sit down and remind them of the basics. Tell them the kinds of questions that predators ask, remind them that downloading music and movies is illegal (and as a parent can actually cost you thousands in legal bills). I've included some tips for teens on the next page. You may want to read it over with your son or daughter.

2. Place the computer in a well trafficked room. If you have young kids (or even teens), place the computer in a room where you can supervise them. I don't recommend spying on kids, but just them knowing that you can see the screen is enough to deter a lot of things.

3. Learn their IM screen names and add them to your buddy list. Check their profiles often. I've shocked friends and family with some of the things I've seen in their kid's AOL Instant Messenger profiles.

4. Visit your child's MySpace, LiveJournal, Xanga, , Friendster, BuddyPic, or Orkut profile. Don't think of this as an invasion of privacy, it's not. These profiles can be viewed by anybody on the web (including predators and potential employers) so anything posted on them is done without an expectation of privacy.

Ryan's Tips For Teens

1. If you wouldn't be comfortable putting your actions, pictures, or words on a billboard in front of your school, don't put them on the internet. Remember, everything you post on the internet can be permanently stored. Do you really want your next job interviewer to see pictures of you hitting the bong in your underwear?

2. Don't give out personal information to people you don't know. Even simple things like the name of your school and the sports you play can be enough for somebody to find you. Too many teens post their cell phone numbers in their IM profiles. Are you comfortable giving your cell phone number to a child predator?

3. Don't meet people from the internet. It's very easy for anybody to pretend to be whoever they want to be on the web, and there's no way to verify it. Just because somebody's profile says they're 14 doesn't mean they really are. Most predators are really good actors and know exactly what to say to make you believe them.

4. Downloading songs, movies, and games without paying for them IS illegal and people DO get caught, so be careful. Is that $10 CD really worth the $10,000 in legal fees your parents could face if you get caught?

5. Tell your parents if you ever feel suspicious about somebody, and ask them before you give out any personal information.

Commonly Misused Words

An argument can be made that thanks to internet slang and text messaging, overall language skills are declining. Many of today's teens have trouble picking which version of a homonym to use (let alone trying to spell homonym).

To help with this, I've compiled a list of some of the most commonly misused words.

Accept, Except - *Accept* means to receive, *except* means to exclude.
Affect, Effect - An *Effect* is a result, *Affect* usually means to alter.
Alright - This isn't a word. You should use **all right**.
Assure, Ensure, Insure - *Assure* means to guarantee, *Ensure* means to make sure, and *Insure* is about insurance
Compliment, Complement - A *Compliment* is praise, to *Complement* is to go well with something else.
Could Of - This doesn't make sense. Use **Could Have**.
Discreet, Discrete - *Discreet* is to be careful, *Discrete* means distinct.
Farther, Further - *Farther* refers to distance, *Further* means more.
Foreword, Forward - A *Foreword* is in a book, *Forward* is the front.
i.e , e.g - In Latin *i.e* means "that is", while *e.g* means "for example".
Its, It's - *Its* is possessive, (belongs to someone) *It's* is short for **it is**.
Labtop, Laptop - *Labtop* is not a word. Computers sit on your lap.
Loose, Lose - *Loose* is not tight, *Lose* is the opposite of win.
Precede, Proceed – *Precede* means come first, *proceed* means follow
Than, Then - *Than* is for comparisons, *Then* means it came next.
There, Their, They're - *There* is a place, *Their* is something that belongs to them, *They're* is short for They Are
To, Too - *Too* means also, *To* is used with verbs (going to).
Weather, Whether - *Weather* for rain or snow, *Whether* is for making a choice.
Who's, Whose - *Whose* is possessive, *Who's* is short for who is.
Your, You're - *Your* is something that belongs to you, *You're* is short for you are.

Acknowledgements

Writing a book is no easy process (even when most of the content is user submitted). This was certainly a learning experience for me and one that I'd gladly (and just may) repeat again.

With that said, there are several people without whom I couldn't have imagined doing this. I'd like to say thank you to the following people:

The Morton Kids (Ashleigh, Paige, Nick, and Amanda) for their constant spelling errors and slang usage that prompted me to make NoSlang.com in the first place.

The NoSlang.com site visitors for submitting many of the words that make up the database (and this book).

Ken Leebow for teaching me about the publishing world and allowing me to bounce ideas off of him. Also, for being the site's #1 promoter.

Yahoo site of the month editors and Kim Komando for their recommendations of the website that sent traffic my way.

Jeff, Scott, Renee, and everybody else who pointed out all my mistakes.

Jon for putting up with my constant cover revisions.

And of course my parents and grandparents who've always supported me in everything I've done.

Printed in the United Kingdom
by Lightning Source UK Ltd.
135708UK00001B/327/A

9 781847 287526